jewish holiday treats

jewish holiday treats

recipes and crafts for the whole family

by joan zoloth

photographs by lisa hubbard

CHRONICLE BOOKS

SAN FRANCISCO

Library of Congress Cataloging-in-Publication Data available.

ISBN 0-8118-2915-4

Printed in Hong Kong.

Food styling by Susan Ottaviano.
Prop and craft styling by Susan Ottaviano and Lisa Hubbard.
Lisa and Susan would like to thank all the people who helped and advised us:
Mordecai Nichols, Annichelle Saludo, Andrea Boone, Bobby Montwaid, Alex White,
Chani Yammer, Barry Singer, Madie and Jake Katz, and Misha and Scout.

Designed by Carrie Leeb and Laura Lovett.
Composition by Suzanne Scott.

Distributed in Canada by Raincoast Books
9050 Shaughnessy Street
Vancouver, British Columbia V6P 6E5

10 9 8 7 6 5 4 3 2 1

Chronicle Books LLC
85 Second Street
San Francisco, California 94105

www.chroniclebooks.com

Notice: This book is intended as an educational and informational guide. With any craft project, check product labels to make sure that the materials you use are safe and nontoxic. Nontoxic is a description given to any substance that does not give off dangerous fumes or contain harmful ingredients (such as chemicals or poisons) in amounts that could endanger a person's health.

Dedication

For my children, with all my love, for their joy and support and never-ending patience with their mom; and for my parents, for all their nurturing and guidance; and Auntie Martha, for love and energy and family sayings.

And of course to Andy—for being supportive in all ways—I thank you.

Acknowledgments

To Marissa Schwartz, for sharing her computer and her dad with me. Unending thanks to the best friend a person could have, Sandra Clement—without her this book couldn't have been written. In deep gratitude to Dan Dorfman for making sure all was "kosher." To nephews Noah and Mat—the best on earth; and their mom—my sister Laurie—for her ideas. And to Uncle Steve, for being the most wonderful person and brother; and to his family Kathy, Emma, and Sam, for happy summers in Vinalhaven. To those at Chronicle Books: Bill LeBlond—my heartfelt thanks for everything; and Leslie Jonath, my editor, for her energy and excitement with the project.

Finally, in memory of my grandparents and Aunt Bessie, whom I miss.

table of contents

introduction

We make our way up the path; I am clutching my menorah. The sun is flashing gold as it begins to set over the mountains. My Aunt Bessie beckons us inside, where the walls are decorated with dreidels and the air is redolent with latkes. My grandfather takes the menorah I made that day and places it among the other menorahs of his children and grandchildren. Together, we light the Chanukah candles and say our quiet prayer. Then, we burst into a rousing chorus of the dreidel song. Presents are searched for, brought forward, and exchanged amidst excited exclamations and thank yous. It is a festive time, lit by the glow of the Chanukah candles.

Holidays are an important way to strengthen the ties that bind families. Each Jewish holiday offers us symbols and rituals that surround the holiday meal. It provides ceremonies that renew the human spirit and a framework in which we layer history and meals together. All of these ceremonies are celebrated in some way by Jews throughout the world.

For me, lighting a menorah at Chanukah or making any other holiday treat is a link to the past and a celebration of my roots. Every family has its own special traditions and dishes for celebrating Jewish occasions.

My goal in writing *Jewish Holiday Treats* is to pass on some ideas for celebrating the holidays, in hopes that you may want to incorporate new traditions with the old. In these pages, you'll find six chapters, each featuring one of the major holidays, and offering up recipes for delicious foods as well as fun projects that the whole family can enjoy.

A dinner of Round-and-Round Challah, Roast Chicken with Rice and Fruit Stuffing, and Amazing Honey Cake starts off the Jewish New Year with a wonderful feast. A Hand-Painted Honey Bowl and Gingerbread Sukkah are projects that your children will enjoy making as they learn about the significance of Rosh Hashanah and Sukkot, respectively. A plentiful Chanukah feast features Traditional Chicken Soup, two ways to make Latkes, and Momma's Beef Brisket with Fruit, while holiday projects include two ways to Make Your Own Menorah and instructions on how to play a game of dreidel. A Passover celebration takes its cue from the bounty of spring and treats the family to such dishes as New Parsley Potatoes, Lamb Shanks with Vegetables, Asparagus with Garlic Sauce, and, for dessert, the fanciful Coconut Pyramids of Egypt. The Jumping Paper Frogs and Stained Glass for Elijah will have everyone participating joyously in the celebration.

Sharing our lives and our history brings to life the ethics, insights, and wisdom of our Jewish heritage and offers moments of celebration and insight for every member of the family. All the food and projects on these pages are meant to entice both the young ones and the young at heart.

Note: The recipes have been created in the kosher style; however, readers should consult with their own rabbis with particular questions.

tips for cooking with kids

* Wash hands thoroughly with soap and water.

* Tie on aprons and tie back long hair.

* Before beginning to cook, read the recipe aloud. Put all the necessary ingredients and tools (including pots and pans) on the table or counter.

* Make sure that the counter you are using is a good height for your children. It should come to their waists. Have a small stool on hand for them if they need to reach a higher counter.

* Do all cutting on a cutting board. If your children are old enough to use a knife, teach them to cut away from their bodies. Set knives, graters, and peelers out of reach until they're ready to use, and wash each sharp utensil separately after using it.

* Don't let pot handles stick out. Turn them in toward the back of the stove, so that you or the little ones won't bump into them or catch them with a sleeve.

* Keep pot holders handy.

tips for crafting with kids

* Read through all the directions before you begin. Stock up on supplies in advance. You might want to keep certain basic items—scissors, paper, tape, colored pencils and crayons, and glue—around the house for last-minute craft whims and rainy days.

* Make sure your workspace is easy to clean, well lit, and well ventilated.

* Line your table or work surface with a plastic drop cloth or waxed paper. I also like to do some craft projects on big baking trays.

* Have paper towels and a damp sponge on hand.

* Have a selection of old, oversized T-shirts or aprons to slip on over clothing as a layer of protection. Tie back loose hair.

* Read the craft instructions aloud with your children. Explain the safety factors that allow an adult to use certain tools that a child may not use. Make sure you have all the materials you need before beginning the project.

Rosh Hashanah, Hebrew for "the Head of the Year," falls in early autumn and marks the beginning of the Jewish calendar. The Jewish New Year begins officially at sunset and the celebration lasts for two days. It is a happy time of wishes for a good year ahead, and the foods eaten during the holiday have special meaning. Sweet dishes like Teeny-Tiny Shofar Cookies and Amazing Honey Cake signify hope for a sweet year. Round-and-Round Challah is shaped into a circle to symbolize a good year all around.

rosh hashanah and yom kippur

The simple projects in this chapter are fun for the whole family to make. Sending handmade New Year's Cards is a traditional way to extend best wishes to family and friends. The Hand-Painted Honey Bowl decorates the table, creating a special honey vessel in which to dip the challah. Lighting the Jelly Jar Candles with the family is the perfect time to say Shanah Tovah!—Happy New Year! You can also decorate your dinner table with a centerpiece of pomegranates, figs, and apples, artfully arranged on a platter. Each seed of the pomegranate, a biblical fruit, symbolizes a good deed to be done in the new year. In fact, some say that the fruit contains 613 seeds—the same number of commandments in the Torah. The others are "new fruits," and it is customary to eat a new fruit—one not yet eaten that season—at Rosh Hashanah.

Ten days after Rosh Hashanah is Yom Kippur, the Jewish Day of Atonement. This day of fasting and prayer is the time when we make amends, a time for forgiveness, and for moving past our mistakes. To help get rid of our wrongdoings over the past year, my sister Laurie and I wrote them down on bits of paper and threw them into the backyard stream. Younger children tore off pieces of bread and threw them into the water. Then we all hugged each other and started the year afresh.

round-and-round challah

There is no better way to begin the year than with this warm egg bread, shaped in a round to represent a well-rounded year ahead. Little hands can help shape the loaves and sprinkle the tops with sesame or poppy seeds. At serving, place a bowl of honey in the center of the round for dipping pieces of the bread.

Yields 2 loaves

In a large bowl, dissolve the yeast and 1 tablespoon of the sugar in the warm milk. Stir in the remaining sugar, the salt, eggs, and oil or margarine. Stir in the flour, 1 cup at a time. Turn out onto a floured board and knead until you can form a smooth ball, about 10 minutes. If the dough is sticky, add a little more flour. Place the dough in an oiled bowl, turn the dough to coat the surface with oil, cover the bowl, and let the dough rise until doubled in size, about 30 to 60 minutes.

Turn the dough out onto a floured work surface and divide it in half. Cover half of the dough with a towel. Divide the other half into 3 equal parts. Roll each part back and forth on the work surface until it forms a rope 24 inches long. Braid the 3 ropes together as you would braid hair. Pinch the ends together to seal. Repeat with the remaining half of the dough.

Line a large, heavy baking sheet with aluminum foil. Oil the foil and sprinkle with yellow cornmeal. Remove the label from a 10-ounce can and wash the can thoroughly. Oil it on the outside and place it in the center of one-half of the baking sheet, open end up. Transfer 1 braid to the baking sheet, forming it into a ring around the can. Join and pinch together the ends of the braid. Remove the can, leaving the braided ring.

continued

2 packages yeast

$^3/_4$ cup sugar

2 cups warm milk
(80° to 100° F)

1 tablespoon salt

5 large eggs, lightly beaten

$^1/_2$ cup vegetable oil or melted margarine

7 cups bread flour or all-purpose flour, or as needed

yellow cornmeal, for coating pan

1 egg, well beaten, for egg wash

sesame or poppy seeds

Repeat with the other braid, placing it on the other half of the baking sheet. Cover the rings with a towel and let them rise in a warm place until doubled in size, about 30 minutes.

Preheat the oven to 350° F.

Brush the braids with the egg wash, and sprinkle with the sesame or poppy seeds. Bake for 30 to 40 minutes, or until golden brown. Let cool on a rack.

israeli salad

4 tomatoes, diced

½ English cucumber, cut into ½-inch dice

1 small yellow or red bell pepper, cut into ½-inch dice

2 green onions, thinly sliced

1 tablespoon coarsely chopped fresh parsley

3 tablespoons fresh lemon juice

2 tablespoons extra-virgin olive oil

¾ teaspoon salt

¼ teaspoon pepper

A friend from Israel once brought this gorgeous early autumn tomato salad to our New Year's dinner. It comes from the kibbutzim, where it is eaten at break after members have put in some time in the fields. You can add a colorful twist by using heirloom tomatoes instead of plain red varieties.

Serves 4

In a bowl, mix all the ingredients together well. Served chilled or at room temperature.

roast chicken with rice and fruit stuffing

4 tablespoons vegetable oil

1 small onion, chopped

1 cup long-grain rice

1¼ cups hot water

½ cup fresh orange juice

salt and pepper to taste

½ cup raisins

1 small apple, peeled, cored, and finely diced

¼ teaspoon ground cinnamon

1 roasting chicken, 3½ to 4 pounds

Stuffed with sweet apple chunks and raisins, this delicious roast chicken will warm up a cool New Year's night.

Serves 4

Preheat the oven to 400° F.

Heat 3 tablespoons of the oil in a deep skillet or sauté pan over low heat, add the onion, and cook until tender, about 5 minutes. Add the rice and sauté over medium heat for about 2 minutes, stirring constantly. Add the hot water and orange juice, season with salt and pepper, and bring to a boil. Reduce the heat to low, cover, and cook for 10 minutes.

Add the raisins and apple to the rice mixture and stir lightly with a fork. Cover and cook until the rice is nearly tender, about 5 minutes. Stir in the cinnamon and taste for seasoning.

Sprinkle the chicken with salt and pepper on all sides. Spoon enough of the rice mixture into the chicken to fill it without packing it too tightly; reserve the extra stuffing. Truss closed. Set the chicken in a roasting pan and bake until the juices run clear when a thigh is pierced, about 1 hour. Remove from the oven and let stand for 5 to 10 minutes before carving.

Meanwhile, heat the remaining tablespoon of oil in a skillet and add the reserved rice stuffing. Cook, stirring, until the rice is tender and the stuffing is heated through. Combine with the stuffing from the chicken cavity and serve alongside the chicken.

amazing honey cake

Traditionally eaten on Rosh Hashanah, honey cake has been traced back at least as far as the Middle Ages. I must admit I hated honey cake as a child. It was always so dense and dry, and where was the frosting? Then I tried my cousin's version of this traditional Rosh Hashanah dessert. After one bite, I proclaimed it "amazing."

Yields 1 cake, serves 12

Preheat the oven to 350° F. Oil an 11-by-14-inch baking dish.

In a large bowl, beat the honey, sugar, vanilla extract, oil, orange juice, orange zest, and melted chocolate until thoroughly blended. Add the eggs and beat until the mixture is light and smooth. In another large bowl, stir together the flour, baking powder, baking soda, cinnamon, salt, and nutmeg. Gradually add the wet ingredients into the flour mixture, beating until smooth.

Pour the batter into the prepared pan. Bake until a toothpick inserted in the center of the cake comes out clean, about 1 hour. Remove from the oven and invert on a rack. With a sharp knife, loosen the cake from the pan sides and center and remove from the pan. Let cool completely on the rack.

½ cup honey

1 cup brown sugar

1 teaspoon vanilla extract

½ cup vegetable oil

1 cup fresh orange juice

zest of 1 orange

2 ounces unsweetened pareve chocolate, melted

3 eggs

3 cups all-purpose flour

¼ teaspoon baking powder

1 teaspoon baking soda

1 teaspoon ground cinnamon

1 teaspoon salt

½ teaspoon ground nutmeg

teeny-tiny shofar cookies

¼ cup (½ stick) unsalted butter

2 tablespoons heavy cream

1 tablespoon orange liqueur

¾ cup almonds, toasted and ground medium-fine

1 tablespoon all-purpose flour

½ cup sugar

Legend says that during Yom Kippur, the gates of Heaven are open and our thoughts and prayers fly straight to God's ears. At the end of the holiday, the shofar—a musical instrument made of a ram's horn—blasts and our Lord calls. These delicious cookies are baked in the shape of tiny shofars. What they actually look like mostly depends on how skilled you are at rolling them when they're hot. This is a good project to do with kids, because the cookies are simple to make and fun to shape. You can also dip them in chocolate, and although they lose the shofar shape, they are still mighty tasty. Because these cookies are made with butter, they should only be served with a dairy meal or alone as a great snack.

Yields 20 cookies

Preheat the oven to 375° F.

In a small saucepan over medium heat, combine the butter, cream, and liqueur. When the butter has melted, stir in the remaining ingredients. Cook until gently bubbling, 2 to 3 minutes. Remove from the heat and keep warm.

Line a baking sheet with parchment. Using a teaspoon measure, drop 5 spoonfuls of batter 1½ inches apart on the prepared baking sheet. Bake until lightly browned and crisp, 6 to 7 minutes. Remove from the oven and let sit until firm enough to handle but still pliable, 1 to 2 minutes. Working quickly, lay each cookie around the handle of a wooden spoon, pressing the edges together to form a cylinder, and leave for 10 seconds, then transfer to a rack to cool. Continue baking and forming cookies until the batter is used up.

jelly jar candles

There is nothing more comforting than holiday lights, and candle lighting is an important part of Jewish religion. Candles have a way of making a moment special. This project is appropriate for adults, but children can help sing the blessings.

Use the scissors to cut the wicks to approximately 3 inches longer than the height of the jars. Attach each wick to a metal wick tab, and fix the tab to the bottom of a jar with a pea-sized piece of putty. Gently pull up each wick and tie to a pencil so that the pencil rests across the top of each jar, the wick is taut, and the tab rests on the bottom of the jar.

Bring water to a boil in the bottom pan of a double boiler, and then place the beeswax in the upper pan. Using the thermometer, heat to 135° F. Remove from the heat. Carefully pour the wax into the jars, taking care not to dislodge the pencils. Use a pot holder to set the jars in a cold water bath to cool. When completely cool, untie the wicks from the pencils and cut them to ½ inch above the wax.

For 4 candles you will need:

scissors

4 wicks

ruler

4 jelly jars (½-pint capacity)

4 metal wick tabs

plumber's or wick putty

4 pencils

double boiler

1½ pounds bleached beeswax

candy thermometer

pot holder

bucket or bowl for water bath

hand-painted honey bowl

Honey takes on a special meaning during Rosh Hashanah, and my aunt had a honey bowl she used just for special occasions. We would dip our slices of apple or challah into the honey and say, "May it be a good, sweet year."

Cover a flat work area with waxed paper so that the sheets overlap, completely protecting the table from spatters and spills. Pour about 1 tablespoon of the paint into the flat dish or plastic lid.

Set the glass bowl upside down on the waxed paper. Dip the brush into the paint and decorate the bowl with the Star of David or autumnal leaves, or make stripes on or below the rim.

After the paint has dried completely, spray the outside of the bowl with clear acrylic. Be sure to do this in a well-ventilated area. Let dry. This bowl should always be washed by hand.

For each bowl you will need:

waxed paper

1 bottle (2 ounces) navy blue acrylic paint

flat dish or plastic lid

1 clear glass bowl

paintbrush, 1/4 inch wide

clear acrylic spray

new year's cards

For 2 cards you will need:

pencil

large white-gum artists' erasers

cookie cutter(s) (optional)

X-Acto knife

1 sheet (9 by 12 inches)
   white or light-colored
   construction paper

pen

large ink pads or gouache paints

Homemade Rosh Hashanah cards are an extra-special way to send Happy New Year wishes to family and friends. First, decide on your message. For example, you can write Leshanah Tovah Umetukah—*"May you have a good and sweet year"—or simply* Shanah Tovah—*"Happy New Year!" Or you might pen the Yiddish* Gut Yontif, Gut Yohr—*"Have a good holiday, have a good year." Designs that reflect the symbols of the holiday, such as pomegranates, jars of honey, or a shofar, are good ideas, as are religious images, such as the Star of David, or perhaps something autumnal, to reflect the season. Little ones will have fun stamping the designs, but grown-ups should handle the X-Acto knife.*

Use the pencil to draw a design onto the flat surface of an eraser. This can be done free hand or by using a cookie cutter as a template and tracing around it. Following the lines on the eraser, cut out the designs with the X-Acto knife. Cut slowly but with enough pressure to make clear cuts and clean shapes. Pull the cut pieces away.

To make the cards, fold the construction paper in half widthwise, then, using the X-Acto, cut it in half along the fold line. Fold each cut piece in half widthwise, creasing it along the folded edge. Use the pen to write a message on the inside of each card.

Use the cutouts as stamps, either pressing them into ink pads or dipping them into gouache paints. If using paint, first pour a small amount (about 2 tablespoons) into a small bowl and thin it with an equal amount of water. You can either stamp your design in one place on the card, such as the center, or in a random pattern.

Note: If you are designing a word stamp be sure to cut out a mirror image.

Rosh Hashanah and Yom Kippur are celebrated in early fall—usually in October—and they culminate with the eight-day festival of Sukkot. On Rosh Hashanah, we discover and begin again. On Yom Kippur, we reconcile with God and with each other. At the end we celebrate Sukkot, the harvest festival of joy and redemption.

sukkot, the feast of tabernacles

The Sukkot recipes in this chapter include a delicious Southern Chicken, a Red Pepper Salad, Noodle Kugel, and a Sephardic Orange Sponge Cake. You may want to celebrate by building a sukkah—an outdoor hut topped with gathered twigs, branches, seasonal fruits, and vines—and hosting your holiday feast inside it. The sukkah symbolizes the desert shelters that Jewish people built when they fled Egypt. My grandfather constructed his sukkah in a potting shed in his backyard. He covered the open ceiling with palm fronds and tied fresh fruit to the branches. The smell of the fruit infused the air as we ate the holiday meal in our small shelter. You can create a festive ambience in your sukkah with Sukkot Spice Balls, Sukkot Squash Candles, and Sukkah String Decorations.

sukkah string decorations

For each decoration you will need:

4 family photos

scissors

glue stick

four 3-by-5-inch index cards or pieces of construction paper

paper punch

1 ribbon, approximately 42 inches long, cut into six 7-inch pieces

light fishing line

needle with big eye

2 large bags cranberries

seasonal leaves (optional)

Traditionally, sukkahs have been decorated with the pictures of ancestors. You can make family photo cards to hang on your string decorations.

Use a photocopy machine to make copies of the photos. Use the scissors to cut out the copies and glue each to a separate index card. Punch a hole at the top of each card and tie each with a ribbon, leaving on the excess. Set the photo cards aside.

Cut a piece of fishing line 6 feet long and tie a knot at one end. Slip the needle onto the other end, then thread on the cranberries and leaves, if using, until the line is full. Tie the photo cards onto the line and hang from the sukkah ceiling in a decorative fashion.

sukkot spice balls

For 6 spice balls you will need:

wooden skewer

2 boxes whole cloves

6 oranges

Kids love to push the cloves into the oranges! You can put these simple spice balls in your sukkah for a delicious scent, or make a few for a festive centerpiece. Let them dry completely before you put the ball in a sweater drawer or any other enclosed space.

It's easier to insert the cloves if holes are made in the oranges first. The wooden skewer makes a useful tool for this purpose. Stick the pointed ends of the cloves into the oranges. Have fun with the designs (see the photograph on page 26). Space the cloves evenly and put them as close together as possible.

A grouping of the studded oranges makes a festive centerpiece for the table, the cloves scenting the air with their warm holiday fragrance.

southern chicken

As a child in Los Angeles, I thought that all American Jews lived in that city or New York, but in Charleston and Savannah, Sephardic Jews can be traced back to the 1700s. Many of the foods they prepared were traditional recipes from the Iberian peninsula, and many of the Jewish traditions became mixed with Southern ones.

Mrs. Franz, who gave me this recipe, was the consummate Southern belle, with a lilting accent, charm, and a clever wit. Best of all, she made a great fried chicken. Unlike the traditional version from the South, this chicken is not fried in lard, but in oil. If you use boneless chicken breasts in the recipe, you can cut them into strips.

Serves 6 to 8

1 teaspoon salt

1 clove garlic, mashed

2 teaspoons sweet paprika

2 frying chickens, cut into 8 pieces each

$1/2$ cup fresh orange juice

$1/4$ cup bourbon

$1/4$ cup water

2 large eggs

$1 1/2$ cups all-purpose flour

vegetable oil for frying

Mix the salt, garlic, and paprika in a small bowl. Place the chicken in a bowl and sprinkle with the spices. In another small bowl, mix the orange juice, bourbon, and water, then pour most of the liquid over the chicken, reserving 2 tablespoons. Cover and refrigerate for several hours or overnight, turning several times.

Drain and dry the chicken. Beat the eggs in a bowl and add the remaining marinade. Place the flour in another bowl. Roll the chicken pieces in the flour, then in the egg mixture, and then in the flour again. Heat oil to a depth of about 4 inches in a heavy pot over high heat. Slip several pieces of the chicken into the hot oil, giving them ample room, and brown for about 6 minutes. Turn over and continue to cook until browned and cooked through, another 4 to 6 minutes. Transfer to paper towels to drain; keep warm. Cook the remaining chicken in the same way and serve piping hot.

red pepper salad

Variations on this Moroccan dish are prepared all around the Mediterranean. The use of eggplant in Jewish recipes traces its origin back to Spain, and when the Jews fled the Inquisition, they took their recipes for this member of the nightshade family to their new homes in North Africa and the Middle East.

Serves 6 to 8

Preheat the oven to 400° F.

Place the eggplant, cut sides down, on a baking sheet and bake until soft, about 40 minutes. Set the eggplant aside on a plate and peel when cool enough to handle. Place the peppers, cut sides down, on the baking sheet and place in the oven until the skins are slightly charred, about 10 minutes. The peppers can also be charred under a broiler, but watch the process closely to avoid overcharring. Transfer the peppers to a plate and let cool, then scrape off the charred skin with a paring knife. The charred peppers can also be placed in a tightly closed paper bag or a covered pot until cool to make peeling easier. Put the tomatoes in boiling water for 1 to 2 minutes, transfer to a plate, peel immediately, halve, and seed.

Cut the eggplant, peppers, and tomatoes into cubes and transfer to a bowl. Add the oil, lemon juice, onion, garlic, salt, pepper, and half of the parsley. Toss to coat. Sprinkle with the remaining parsley. Serve warm or at room temperature with the pita bread.

1 eggplant (about 1 pound), halved lengthwise

1 large green bell pepper, halved and seeded

1 large red bell pepper, halved and seeded

4 or 5 tomatoes (about 1 pound)

3 tablespoons extra-virgin olive oil

2 tablespoons fresh lemon juice

1 medium onion, finely chopped

3 cloves garlic, minced

salt and pepper to taste

1/2 cup coarsely chopped fresh Italian parsley

pita bread, cut in wedges and heated

noodle kugel

12 ounces flat, wide egg noodles

½ cup (1 stick) margarine

2 apples, peeled, cored, and diced

½ cup golden raisins, rinsed

4 eggs, beaten

salt to taste

cinnamon sugar for sprinkling

Many Jewish cooks treasure recipes for this ubiquitous dish that have been handed down through generations. Kugels can be made savory for a side dish or sweet for a dessert. I've tasted kugels with crunchy tops and soft tops, with cheese or pineapple. There is the potato kugel and the noodle kugel, and each of these in turn has its own variations. But best of all, kids love kugel—especially the noodle version. This sweet version is typical of an Ashkenazic or Eastern European kitchen. This will make a generous portion, but leftovers are delicious the next day.

Serves 10 to 12

Preheat the oven to 375° F. Generously grease a 9-by-13-inch baking dish.

Bring a large saucepan of lightly salted water to a boil, add the noodles, and boil until al dente, 5 to 10 minutes. Drain and place in a large bowl. Add the margarine, apples, and raisins and mix well. Add the eggs, season with salt, and mix well. Spoon the mixture into the prepared baking dish. Sprinkle with cinnamon sugar.

Bake until the top is brown and crisp, 35 to 45 minutes. Remove from the oven and serve hot or cold, cut into squares.

sephardic orange sponge cake

This ultralight cake is infused with orange. The Jews were known as prolific propagators of citrus in the Mediterranean during the Middle Ages. Later, Jewish traders sold oranges and lemons throughout the world. Because of the importance of oranges in the Sephardic world, hundreds of recipes for their use exist. Although traditionally made without icing, this typical Sephardic cake receives a glaze in this featherlight version.

Serves 8 to 10

Preheat the oven to 325° F.

In a bowl, beat the egg whites until foamy. Add the cream of tartar and ½ cup of the sugar. Beat until stiff and shiny but not dry. In another bowl, beat the egg yolks with the remaining 1 cup sugar until light and fluffy. Gently fold the yolk mixture into the beaten whites. Gradually fold in the flour and orange juice. Do not overmix.

Pour the batter into an ungreased 10-inch tube pan with a removable bottom. Bake for 50 minutes. Increase the temperature to 350° F and bake until the cake springs back when touched and a toothpick inserted into the center comes out clean, 5 to 10 minutes. Allow to cool in the pan for 30 minutes, then loosen the cake from the sides and center of the pan and unmold onto a serving platter.

To make the glaze, combine the orange juice, orange zest, and sugar in a small saucepan and heat until dissolved. Pour it over the warm cake.

7 eggs, separated

½ teaspoon cream of tartar

1½ cups sugar

1½ cups sifted all-purpose flour

½ cup fresh orange juice

Glaze:

½ cup fresh orange juice

grated zest of 1 orange

2 teaspoons granulated sugar

sukkot squash candle

Autumn fruits and vegetables are key elements of the harvest celebration, and it's fun to create crafts with them as well as to cook with them. This recipe uses a squash as a mold for a unique candle, and although it calls for an acorn squash, it can be made with other beautiful varieties, such as white pumpkin or patty pan. The texture of the squash's interior will leave interesting, deep-ridged patterns on your candle.

First, hollow out the squash. Use the knife to cut the top off, the way you would for a pumpkin used as a jack-o'-lantern. Using a metal spoon, remove the seeds and string.

Thread the needle with the wick. Pierce the bottom of the squash with the needle, pushing it all the way through the flesh and out through the top of the squash. Tie a knot at the end of the wick that sticks out from the bottom of the squash. If there is excess space between the wick and the flesh, fill it with a little bit of putty.

Heat the paraffin in the top pan of the double boiler over simmering water. Tie the top of the wick to a pencil and lay the pencil across the top of the squash. When melted, pour the paraffin into the empty squash, keeping some in reserve. As it cools, top it off with a bit more paraffin if necessary. You can leave the candle in the squash holder or, when the paraffin has hardened, cut away the squash shell. If you cut away the squash, flatten the base of your candle by rubbing it in an old skillet over low heat.

For each candle you will need:

1 acorn squash

sharp knife

metal spoon

long upholstery needle

1 wick

putty

double boiler

paraffin (amount depends on
    the size of the squash used)

pencil

old skillet

gingerbread sukkah

Gingerbread:

6 cups all-purpose flour

1 teaspoon baking soda

½ teaspoon baking powder

1 cup (2 sticks) margarine

1 cup dark brown sugar

4 teaspoons ground ginger

4 teaspoons ground cinnamon

1½ teaspoons ground cloves

1½ teaspoons salt

1 large egg

1½ cups unsulfured molasses

Icing:

3 large egg whites

5 cups (1¼ pounds) powdered
   sugar

Roof:

twigs

small, leafy branches

During their escape from Egypt, the Jews sought shelter in temporary huts known as sukkahs, the same structures that farmers slept in to be near their crops during the harvest season. If you can't make a large, sit-in sukkah (see page 27), create this small version as a centerpiece for your dining table.

Yields enough for 1 house

To make the gingerbread, in a large bowl sift together the flour, baking soda, and baking powder. Set aside. In a separate bowl, cream the margarine and brown sugar until fluffy. Mix in the spices and salt. Beat in the egg and molasses. Stir in the flour mixture until combined. Wrap the dough in plastic wrap. Chill for at least 1 hour.

On a well-floured board, roll out the dough ⅛ inch thick. Cut into 4 same-sized rectangles to create the four walls of a sukkah. In one of the rectangles cut a smaller rectangle for the door. Place all of the rectangles on an ungreased baking sheet and chill until firm, about 20 minutes. Meanwhile, preheat the oven to 350° F. Bake until the ginger-bread is firm in the center but not dark around the edges, about 15 minutes. Cool on a wire rack.

To make the icing, beat the egg whites with an electric mixer on medium speed until just frothy. Beat in ¼ cup of the powdered sugar until thick. Add the remaining sugar and beat on high speed until the icing holds a firm peak. Cover with a damp paper towel and set aside until ready to use.

Cement the house pieces together with icing. When dry, make the roof with twigs and small pieces of greenery. You can use the icing to attach trim as well.

A candle burning in a menorah is the quintessential Chanukah moment. Tradition tells of a Jerusalem temple that was defiled by idol worship and later recaptured by Judah Maccabee and his soldiers, who, seeking to rededicate it to the worship of God, cleaned and repaired it. A young boy found a jar of oil to light its lamp, but there was only enough for one day. Miraculously, the lamp burned for eight nights. Today,

chanukah, festival of lights

all over the world, Jewish families light candles in the menorah—a nine-branched candelabra—to celebrate the miracle of the burning lamp and religious freedom.

There are many traditions associated with Chanukah, including warm meals, decorations, dreidels, and menorahs. Latkes, Traditional Chicken Soup, Kids' Applesauce, and Momma's Beef Brisket with Fruit make up my version of the Chanukah meal. Chanukah Star Cookies are a sweet finish, and the kids will love to help cut them out.

Craft projects such as Yummy Chanukah Gelt, Make Your Own Menorah, and Wrap-It-Up Chanukah will keep your children happily occupied throughout the eight days, and will teach them to commemorate the miracle that Chanukah represents.

make your own menorah

The Chanukah menorah (hanukkiyyah) *has nine branches, one for each of the eight nights of the holiday and one for the shammes* (shammash), *or server. The eight candleholders should be the same height, with the shammes set above or apart from the rest as a guardian of the lights. The candles are placed in their holders from right to left, but they are lit from the opposite direction. This way, when lighting begins on the left-hand side, you start with that day's candle, then go on to the one for the day before, and so forth. In some families, the youngest child lights the shammes and then recites the blessing while lighting the other candles.*

menorah for the young

For each menorah you will need:

air-dry ceramic clay

bamboo skewers

poster paint(s)

paintbrush

Reading the story of Chanukah will make the festival more meaningful to a young child. You can relate it as your child pounds and pushes the soft clay into a menorah that you can then place next to your own. Put the menorahs in the window, light the candles, and stand with your child in the darkness of the night, watching the lights of Chanukah shine.

Form the clay into a 1-foot-long, 2-inch-thick piece. The shape can be free-form. Have your child push a thumb into the clay nine times, one for each candle. Take a small 1-inch-long piece of clay and roll it out in the palm of your hand to form a long cylinder. Shape the cylinder into a ring and wrap it around a thumbprint to form a holder for the candlestick. Pinch the holder to the menorah. Repeat this step for each of the remaining eight thumbprints. Use several rings of clay for the center candlestick. If the clay becomes too dry while working with it, apply a little water with your fingertips. Use a bamboo skewer to draw designs or engrave a name. Allow 1 to 2 days to dry completely.

After the clay has dried, paint your menorah as desired. Allow the paint to dry before inserting clandles. A parent may have to drip a bit of hot wax in each holder to keep candles in place.

hardware nut menorah

This menorah is made from simple materials. Menorahs can be made by anyone, which is what the rabbis intended. They wanted everyone, no matter how poor, to light Chanukah candles. The diameter of the nuts will depend on whether you want to use traditional Chanukah candles or dinner candles. Buy your candles first and bring them with you to the hardware store.

Cover a worktable with newspapers. With the glue, attach the nuts to the piece of wood, spacing them far enough apart that the flames won't touch one another. You can position the nuts as candleholders in any way you like, but remember to add the shammes holder. It can be higher or lower—just so long as it's set apart in some way.

In a well-ventilated area, spray paint the wood gold or silver. If you want to make it fancier, glue on imitation jewels or shake glitter onto additional dots of glue.

For each menorah you will need:

newspapers

all-purpose white glue

9 hardware nuts, sized at the hardware store to fit your candles

piece of wood, 1 foot long and 2 to 3 inches wide

gold or silver spray paint

imitation jewels (optional)

glitter (optional)

traditional chicken soup

1 large chicken, about 5 pounds

9 cups water

1 large onion, quartered

2 carrots, thickly sliced

1 leek, sliced

1 parsnip, quartered

2 celery stalks and leaves, chopped

1 bay leaf

1/2 cup white wine (optional)

salt and pepper to taste

handful of rice or hand-crushed vermicelli

According to every Jewish mother, chicken soup cures the common cold, if not more. My dad, like many Jews, calls it the "Jewish penicillin." No matter what you call it, it always makes you feel good and loved. The recipe here is a Sephardic version, as rice and pasta are typically used in Sephardic soups. Chicken soup plays a far more important role in Ashkenazic culture and is used as a basis for holiday meals. My dad says a key ingredient in this recipe is the parsnip, since it sweetens the soup.

Serves 8

Place the chicken in a large pan with the water. Bring slowly to a boil, removing scum as it forms. Add the vegetables and bay leaf, reserving some of the celery leaves as garnish. If you like, add the white wine. Season with salt and pepper. Simmer, partially covered, on very low heat for 1 hour, adding water as necessary to maintain original level. Remove the chicken. When cool enough to handle, strip the meat from the bones in large pieces and set aside with a little of the broth to serve as a second course. Return the bones to the pot. Re-cover partially and continue cooking, adding water as needed, for 1 1/2 hours longer.

Strain the broth. Skim the fat off the top. Before serving, add a handful of rice or vermicelli and let simmer until soft. If you wish, return some of the chicken pieces to the soup. Just before serving, taste and adjust the seasoning. Ladle into bowls to serve. Garnish with the reserved celery leaves.

momma's beef brisket with fruit

Whenever I ask my kids what they want me to cook for dinner, they both say brisket. There is nothing better than this rich, flavorful entrée, cooked until so tender it falls apart into shreds. This hearty dish is equally good when you substitute apple juice or beer for the red wine.

Serves 6 to 8

Preheat the oven to 350° F.

In a large skillet, heat the oil over medium heat. Brown the brisket on all sides and set aside. In the same skillet, sauté the garlic and onions until brown. Transfer to a large roasting pot and place the meat on top, fat side up. Pour in half the wine. Cover and bake for 30 minutes.

Remove from the oven. In a bowl, combine the tomato paste, brown sugar, and hot water to make a paste. Spoon this mixture over the brisket. Sprinkle with salt and pepper. Surround the meat with the carrots, parsnips, and the remaining wine.

Reduce the heat to 325° F, cover, and bake until tender, 2½ to 3 hours, adding the prunes during the last 30 minutes. To serve, transfer the brisket to a deep platter and slice against the grain. Arrange the vegetables and fruit over and around the meat.

4 tablespoons olive oil

1 lean brisket of beef, about 8 pounds

2 cloves garlic, minced

5 medium onions, sliced

1½ cups red wine

2 tablespoons tomato paste

2 tablespoons brown sugar

¼ cup hot water

salt and pepper to taste

4 medium carrots, peeled and thickly sliced

2 parsnips, peeled and thickly sliced

¼ pound dried pitted prunes

latkes

One of the most popular Chanukah foods, deep-fried latkes are eaten to commemorate the miracle of the one-day supply of oil that continued to burn for eight days. According to the traditional story, the early Jews made latkes because they were quick to fry and could be prepared and eaten between battles with the Greeks. It is also said that Jewish villagers would fry quick batches of latkes to feed the Maccabees when they came racing through town on their way to do battle with the Syrian army. The traditional Ashkenazic latke, a potato fritter, is the one I grew up with. Over the years, I've attended numerous Chanukah parties, collecting many different recipes. I have enjoyed latkes that are pulverized, held together with matzo meal and fried. I have eaten latkes as a side dish, as an appetizer, and even as a dessert served with a sprinkle of sugar.

If you are frying latkes for a large gathering, it is helpful to prepare them the day before. Wrap and refrigerate them. Twenty minutes before serving, preheat the oven to 350° F, and warm the latkes for 10 minutes on an ungreased baking sheet.

Alternatively, you can make the latkes well ahead of time and freeze them. To freeze latkes, fry them until they are only slightly brown. Drain and place on a baking sheet that has been lined with kitchen towels and freeze. To serve, put the frozen latkes on a foil-lined baking sheet. Preheat the oven to 400° F and bake until crisp, 5 to 10 minutes.

classic potato latkes

1 small onion

3 russet potatoes

3 tablespoons all-purpose flour

2 eggs, beaten

$1/4$ teaspoon salt

dash of pepper

$1/2$ to 1 cup vegetable oil
  for frying

Have all the ingredients ready to go before you grate the potatoes so they won't discolor. Some people add a pinch of baking soda to prevent them from turning brown.

Yields about 12 pancakes

Coarsely grate the onion into a large bowl. Peel the potatoes and coarsely grate them into the onions. Stir in the flour, eggs, salt, and pepper.

Heat about $1/3$ cup oil in a large skillet over medium-high heat until very hot. Drop heaping tablespoons of the mixture into the oil and flatten with the back of the spoon. Fry, flipping once or twice, until crisp and brown on both sides. Drain on paper towels. Repeat until all the latkes are fried, adding more oil as needed.

latke blinis

Dollar-sized latkes topped with a bit of smoked salmon and crème fraîche can be served as an appetizer during Chanukah with a dairy meal. On their own, they make an elegant hors d'oeuvre any time of the year.

kids' applesauce

This easy recipe is fun to prepare with kids. They can add the cut apples to the apple juice and sugar, and will have fun smashing the cooled apples with a potato masher. The sauce makes a great topping for latkes. It can also be eaten plain, served warm or cold.

Yields 4 cups

Peel the apples if preferred, and cut them into quarters. Place in a heavy pot and add the juice or water and the sugar and lemon juice to taste. Cover the pot and simmer over low heat, stirring often. If the apples begin to stick, add a little more liquid. Cook until the apples are soft.

Let cool a tad. Mash the apples into sauce using a potato masher or run though a food mill. Serve warm, or refrigerate until ready to serve.

2 pounds baking apples, cored

½ cup apple juice or water

2 to 3 tablespoons sugar

juice of 1 lemon, or to taste

chanukah star cookies

No matter what your age, it is always fun to cut out and decorate cookies. Using small rolling pins will make spreading the dough less frustrating for children. I keep an assortment of cookie cutters on hand for all sorts of holiday projects. I sometimes cut out a peanut-butter-and-jelly sandwich with a Star of David cookie cutter for a lunch-box surprise.

Yields about 40 cookies

To make the cookies, in a large bowl, cream the butter and sugar. Beat in the egg. Add the vanilla extract and mix well. Combine the flour, baking powder, and salt in another bowl. Add to the creamed mixture and stir until smooth. Chill the dough for at least 1 hour.

Preheat the oven to 350° F.

Divide the dough into 2 or 3 portions. On a generously floured board, roll out each portion 1/4 inch thick. Cut out shapes using flour-dipped 3-inch cookie cutters and place cookies on ungreased baking sheets. Bake for 5 to 7 minutes, or until edges are lightly browned. Let cool on a rack.

To make the icing, blend the sugar, lemon juice, and water in a bowl. Add more water if needed to thin icing. Divide the icing in half. Add the blue food coloring to one half and mix until the color is uniform. With a small spatula, spread the blue icing evenly over the cooled cookies. Place the white icing in a pastry bag fitted with a star tip and pipe designs as desired.

Cookies:

1 stick unsalted butter

1 cup sugar

1 egg, lightly beaten

1 teaspoon vanilla extract

2 cups all-purpose flour

1/2 teaspoon baking powder

1/4 teaspoon salt

Icing:

2 cups powdered sugar

1 tablespoon lemon juice

1 tablespoon water

2 or 3 drops blue food coloring

yummy chanukah gelt

16 ounces semisweet chocolate

gold or silver metallic paper or aluminum foil, cut into twenty-four 2-inch squares

A big part of celebrating Chanukah is playing dreidel. To play dreidel, you need "gelt," or money. At the time of the Maccabean war, Jewish children were said to have contributed their pennies to the cause of redeeming their people from oppression. You can buy chocolate gelt at the store, but it is much more fun to make your own.

Yields 24 coins

Line a baking sheet with waxed paper. Melt the chocolate in a double boiler over simmering water. When the chocolate is melted, remove the pan from the heat. Spoon coin-sized amounts of chocolate onto the waxed paper. Refrigerate until the chocolate is hard, about 20 minutes. Remove each coin from the waxed paper and wrap it in a paper or foil square.

how to play the dreidel game

The Hebrew letters—nun, gimel, heh, and sh'in—stand for the Hebrew phrase Nes gadolha-ya sham, *or "A great miracle happened there." First, all players put an equal number of items in the pot, such as Chanukah gelt, pennies, or peanuts. Everyone takes a turn spinning the dreidel. If it lands on* nun, *you get nothing. If it lands on* heh, *you get half. If it lands on* sh'in, *you put more in; and if it lands on* gimel, *you get everything in the pot. Then everyone puts the starter amount into the pot again. When you have nothing left, you drop out, and the last survivor wins. You can buy beautiful dreidels in many colors or make the one below.*

Make a copy of the template below. Trace the outline onto a piece of colorful card stock and cut along the solid lines. Draw letters with pen or crayon. Fold along the dotted lines and glue the tabs in place as shown. Insert a 3-inch piece of the straw in the cut X and glue in place. Allow to dry.

template (see below)

1 piece card stock

scissors

pens or crayons

white glue

1 drinking straw

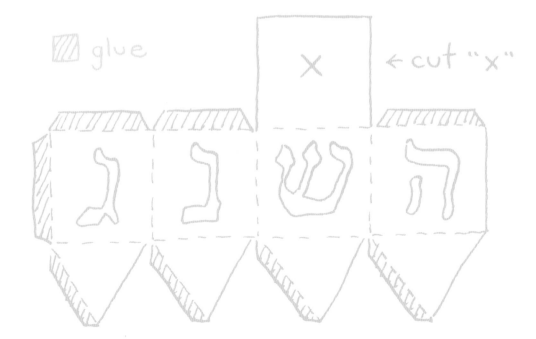

glue

X

← cut "x"

52

wrap-it-up chanukah

Some families give presents every night of Chanukah, while others are more selective. If you do give gifts, homemade Chanukah wrapping paper will make a gift even more unique and special. The paper will be slightly irregular, but, of course, that's its charm. Here, you can make fun Chanukah designs, such as stars, moons, or candles. You could even try to stamp eight candles to make a menorah. Kids will have fun stamping, but parents should always handle sharp cutting tools.

Cut the potato in half crosswise and use the pencil to draw your design onto the flesh. You can also use a cookie cutter to mark your design. Using the X-Acto or paring knife, carve around the outline and cut away the background of your design to a depth of $1/4$ inch. Thin the paints with water if needed. Either paint directly on the design with a brush or dip the potato in a dish of paint, using the dish like a stamp pad. Do a few test prints on newspaper to get rid of excess paint, then print onto the wrapping paper. Let it dry.

large russet potato

large, sharp knife

pencil

chanukah cookie cutters (optional)

X-Acto knife or paring knife

gouache paint or poster paint

paintbrush

dish

long sheet of plain wrapping paper

In the story of Purim, King Ahasuerus of Persia had an evil minister, Haman, who decreed death to all Jews. His wife, Queen Esther, went to him and revealed that she herself was Jewish, and pleaded with him to save the lives of all her people. Her husband rescinded the decree, and Purim is the celebration of that day of survival. Carnivals, parades, and costumes all mark the occasion. During the reading of the

purim, festival of lots

Megillah (The Book of Esther), children sound noisemakers at every mention of the wicked Haman's name. In the past, Jews would write Haman's name on pieces of stone and rub them together until his name was erased.

For children, Purim offers a lesson in giving to others. It is customary to deliver food gifts to neighbors in the spirit of shalah manot, thus fulfilling the biblical command of "sending portions to others." The Purim meal includes many symbolic foods. Fish is eaten to symbolize fertility. Herbs and vegetables remind us that Queen Esther was a vegetarian. Hamantaschen, a triangular stuffed pastry, is said to represent the three-cornered hat worn by Haman.

queen esther crown of flowers

For 1 crown you will need:

measuring tape

florist's wire, 24 inches long

wire cutters

floral tape

scissors

real or fabric flowers

We honor the courage of Queen Esther by dressing up as her for the costume parties that are common to the Purim holiday.

Wrap the measuring tape around your child's head to determine how long the crown should be, allowing two extra inches. Use the wire cutters to trim the wire to size. Bend 1 inch of wire to make a hook at one end and 1 inch of wire to make an eye at the other. Cut a strip of floral tape 12 inches long. Starting at the hooked end, wrap the strip around the wire. Use the scissors to cut the stems of the flowers 2 or 3 inches long. As you wrap the wire with the tape, fasten a flower to the wire by winding the tape around the stem a few times. Face all the flowers in the same direction. Keep cutting strips of tape and adding flowers all along the wire in the same way.

Wrap the finished crown around your child's head. Hook the two ends together and squeeze to fasten the hooks together. Using floral tape, wrap a flower over the hook and eye to hide them.

a very simple crown

For 1 crown you will need:

scissors

1 sheet yellow or gold construction paper

paper punch

1 yard gold yarn

all-purpose white glue

silver or gold glitter

This is a fast, simple variation on the Queen Esther crown that can be cut out of construction paper for a small child to decorate.

Use the scissors and cut a zig-zag across the paper to make two serrated strips. Wrap one of the strips around your child's head and trim to fit. Use a paper punch to make a hole at either end. Tie an 18-inch piece of yarn in each hole. Lay the crown flat and drizzle glue all over it. If the child is too young, you can do this task. Sprinkle glitter on the wet glue. Let dry completely before wearing. To wear, tie the crown around your child's head and tie the yarn in a bow so that the crown fits snugly.

tzedaka box

Purim is a time to give to those less fortunate. Tzedakas, or charity boxes, are used to collect money, and making Tzedakas at home is a lovely way to teach children about giving to worthy causes. You can use a variety of materials to make such a box. Below is one simple and colorful container that can be made in just a few minutes.

Use the measuring tape to measure the height and circumference of the tin. Using the measuring tape and scissors, measure and cut out a rectangle of felt to match the measurements of the tin. Spread glue over the surface of the tin and wrap the rectangle of felt around it. Let dry for at least 1 hour.

You are now ready to decorate your "box" in any number of ways. Glue flat beads to your box to spell out your name or dot with glue and dust with glitter. Attach tiny bouquets of silk flowers or line the box with bells. There are no rules, so have fun.

For each box you will need:

measuring tape

clean, dry baking powder tin, or other similar container

felt in desired color

scissors

white glue

decorations such as flat beads, glitter, bells, miniature silk flowers (optional)

baked halibut with herb butter

Herb Butter:

½ cup (1 stick) unsalted butter,
    at room temperature

2 tablespoons chopped fresh dill

2 tablespoons chopped fresh
    chervil

salt and pepper to taste

½ teaspoon lemon juice

4 small halibut steaks,
    1 to 1½ inches thick

This simple spring dish is adapted from an Eastern European recipe by way of a friend in New England.

Serves 4

Preheat the oven to 425° F.

To make the herb butter, combine the butter, herbs, salt, pepper, and lemon juice in a small bowl. Mix thoroughly. Keep refrigerated until ready to use.

Butter a large baking dish and place in the preheated oven for about 5 minutes. Place the fish steaks in the heated dish. Dot with some of the herb butter. Cover with parchment paper. Bake for about 5 minutes. Remove the parchment paper, dot with more herb butter, and bake for another 5 minutes, or until the meat is white at the bone. Serve immediately.

baked lemon rice with herbs

¼ cup (½ stick) unsalted butter

2 shallots, minced

2 cups long-grain rice

finely grated zest of 2 lemons

leaves from 1 or 2 sprigs fresh
    tarragon

3½ cups vegetable stock

salt and pepper to taste

Rice is a Sephardic staple. The use of rice spread throughout the world as people moved through the Middle East and then into the Mediterranean. Each community added their own twist to the staple, such as a sprinkling of nuts or fresh herbs. Here we add lemon zest to give the dish a festive note.

Serves 6

Preheat the oven to 400° F.

Melt the butter in an ovenproof Dutch oven over medium heat. Add the shallots and sauté until tender, 3 to 4 minutes. Add the rice and cook, stirring, until opaque, 3 to 5 minutes. Stir in half of the lemon zest, half of the tarragon leaves, and all of the stock. Cover, place in the oven, and bake until the stock is absorbed and the rice is tender, 20 to 25 minutes.

Stir in the remaining lemon zest and tarragon leaves and season with salt and pepper. Serve immediately.

cucumber salad

This is a good accompaniment to any meal, since it is light and fresh and easy to make. The large circles of sliced cucumber recall the half shekels (half dollars) of biblical times.

Serves 4 to 6

Peel and slice the cucumbers and place them between paper towels to absorb some of the moisture. Leave them covered until the dressing is ready.

In a small skillet, gently heat the vinegar and basil over low heat for 2 minutes. Pour into a large bowl and add the olive and vegetable oils, mustard, salt, pepper, and sugar. Whisk until thick. Add the cucumbers and toss well. Cover and refrigerate until ready to serve.

2 English cucumbers

3 tablespoons sherry vinegar

1 teaspoon minced basil leaves

3 tablespoons extra-virgin olive oil

3 tablespoons vegetable oil

2 tablespoons Dijon mustard

salt and pepper to taste

$^{1}/_{2}$ teaspoon sugar

hamantaschen

Here, the hamantaschen are stuffed with prune and poppy seed fillings. Poppy seeds commemorate Queen Esther's fast, when she ate only seeds as she prayed for the repeal of the decree.

Dough:

¾ cup sugar

2 cups all-purpose flour

2 teaspoons baking powder

⅓ cup butter or margarine,
    cut into pieces

2 tablespoons water

½ teaspoon vanilla extract

1 egg, beaten

Egg wash:

1 egg, beaten

1 teaspoon water

fillings (recipes follow)

¼ pound pitted prunes

¼ small apple, peeled and grated

1 teaspoon honey

5 tablespoons poppy seeds

1½ tablespoons honey

Yields approximately 20 pastries

Preheat the oven to 350° F. Grease a baking sheet.

Stir together the sugar, flour, and baking powder in a bowl. Add the butter pieces and mix in with a fork until crumbly. Add the water, vanilla extract, and egg. Mix until the dough comes together in a ball.

Sprinkle flour on a work surface and a rolling pin, then flour your hands. Pinch off a piece of dough and roll it into a ball about 1½ inches in diameter. Using the rolling pin, roll out the ball into a round about ⅛ inch thick. Brush with egg wash. Put a teaspoon of filling in the middle of the round. Fold up three edges of the dough and pinch them together to make a triangle. Brush the entire cookie with egg wash. Place on the prepared baking sheet. Repeat with the remaining dough. Bake until light golden at the edges, about 20 minutes. Let cool on a rack.

prune filling

Put the prunes in a pan. Add water to cover. Bring to a boil and cook over medium heat for 20 minutes. Drain and let cool. Chop the prunes, then combine with the apple and honey and mix well.

poppy seed filling

Soak the poppy seeds overnight; drain well. Grind them in a food processor or grinder, add the honey, and mix well.

easy masks

Purim is the time to make believe you are somebody else, so people dress in disguise as the various characters in the story. They might wear masks that depict the faces of King Ahasuerus, Queen Esther, and Haman. It is fun to invite friends over and have a table full of craft supplies from which to make masks. When the masks are completed, you can play marching music or a Purim recording and have your guests parade their costumes.

paper-plate mask

This is a simple mask to make with younger kids. An adult needs to cut out the place for the eyes and nose. You can either fasten the plate around the head of a child with a piece of string, or add a Popsicle stick at the bottom of the plate to use as a handle.

Paint the paper plate in bright, fun colors (you can skip this step if using colored construction paper). When dry, use the scissors to cut out a place for the eyes and nose. Glue on glitter, jewels, or other materials of your choosing. If attaching with string, fit the mask around the head and mark on the back where to tie. Use the paper punch to make holes for the tie. Cut 2 pieces of the string and put them through the holes. Tie on each side and fasten in the middle by tying a bow. If your child prefers to hold the mask in front of his or her face, use the glue to fasten a Popsicle stick to one side of the plate. This makes a handle for holding the mask over the face.

For each mask you will need:

paintbrush

paper plate, or 5-by-8-inch piece
    colored construction paper

acrylic paint, any colors

scissors

glitter, imitation jewels, or other
    decorating materials

paper punch

string or yarn, or Popsicle stick

all-purpose white glue

Passover, the spring holiday of freedom and renewal, commemorates the exodus of the Jews from Egypt and their release from bondage. As the story goes, the pharaohs feared and despised the Jews, enslaving them and forcing them into hard labor, and decreeing that all Jewish baby boys be killed at birth. Moses, spared from this cruel decree, received God's charge to return to Egypt and lead his people to liberation.

passover

He went to the pharaoh and demanded that he release the Jewish people. Moses then threatened that God would bring the plagues to show His power and to punish the pharaoh for not letting the people go. After each plague, the pharaoh was again asked to let the people go. The pharaoh refused until the final plague, which resulted in the death of the first-born in every Egyptian household. Only where an Israelite had slaughtered a lamb and smeared its blood upon the doorpost of his house did the plague of death "pass over" and the first-born survive. Today, every year at the Seder table, Jews read the Haggadah and retell the story of the Israelites' miraculous escape from slavery more than three thousand years ago.

This holiday celebrates the rich shared heritage of thousands of years, passed from one generation to the next at the Seder meal. In this chapter, you'll find recipes for the Seder plate, a festive Passover Dinner, and a festive Passover Breakfast. With so much ceremony attached to the holiday, there are plenty of ways your children can participate. Projects such as a Stained Glass for Elijah, Matzo Place Cards, and a Matzo Cover are fun ways to get the family involved in the Passover celebration. Just as spring adorns the earth, Passover, or Pesach in Hebrew, is a time of the year when your home should shine with beautiful handmade treasures.

the seder plate

The Seder plate holds all the traditional symbols of Passover. Five different foods are included, each with a symbolic meaning.

Karpas—A bit of parsley or other greens. This is the symbol of spring, when everything starts anew.

Z'roa—A roasted lamb shank. The bone symbolizes the Passover sacrifice.

Charoset—A mixture of chopped apples, nuts, and wine. The mixture is a symbol of the mortar used by the Jewish slaves for the pharaoh's buildings.

Marror—A bitter vegetable like horseradish. It is a reminder of the hard and bitter life endured by the slaves.

Beitzah—A hard-boiled egg. The egg symbolizes life.

the afikomen

In addition to the Seder plate, we set the table with a plate holding three matzos, which represent Abraham, Isaac, and Jacob. The middle matzo is broken in half. This broken half is called the afikomen, and it is hidden at the beginning of the meal. At the end of the Seder the children search for the afikomen, for the Seder cannot be finished until it is found. The one who finds it gets a reward. My grandfather always placed it under the napkin by his plate. It was almost a rite of passage, a sign you had grown older, when you figured out his traditional hiding place. When we found the afikomen, my grandfather would, with great ceremony, withdraw his worn leather wallet from his pocket and slowly extract a dollar.

elijah's cup

Elijah was a famous wise man in biblical times. During the Seder we drink four cups of wine or grape juice to symbolize the four promises of redemption in the Book of Exodus. A fifth cup is on the table, too, for the prophet who, according to legend, visits every Jewish home on Passover. Many people use only red wine at the Seder, as a reminder of the blood the Jews smeared on their doorposts to keep their first-born safe during the last of the ten plagues.

stained glass for elijah

Elijah is the biblical prophet who sought justice for the weak against the strong. His glass, therefore, is special and should differ from the other glassware on the table. According to the Haggadah, Elijah is still helping people in need and will someday announce the coming of the messiah.

Using the paintbrush, apply the glue to each bead and attach, one by one, to the base of the wineglass in your desired pattern. Hold beads in place while glue sets. Let beads dry at least 1 hour. Turn glass upside down and continue gluing beads over the cup of the glass. Allow the glass to dry overnight. You will not be able to wash the outside of this glass. Instead, rinse the inside carefully with a sponge.

Note: The beads used in this project are often referred to as flats. Specialty bead shops carry beads in myriad colors and sizes. We used flat beads for our glass.

For each glass you will need:

paintbrush

glue for glass or Duco cement

50 to 100 glass or plastic beads

1 wineglass

71

matzo place cards

For 8 place cards you will need:

8 pieces card stock,
   2 by 4 inches

scissors

2 matzo boxes

all-purpose white glue

Help your guests find their seats at your table.

Fold each piece of card stock in half to form 2-inch square cards that you can stand at a place setting. Cut the paper wrapping off a matzo box and use it to decorate the cards by cutting out individual letters from the words on the paper to spell out the name of each guest. If you cannot find a particular letter, cut a letter from an old magazine or newspaper. Glue the names on the cards and display on the Seder table.

matzo cover

For each cover you will need:

steam iron

needle and thread (optional)

4 feet of fringe

1 piece of fabric,
   12 inches square

felt-tip markers

iron-on patches

scissors

This is a fairly quick project to cover your matzo on the Passover table.

Steam or sew a fringe on all sides of your piece of fabric. Write the word *Matzo* on one or more iron-on patches. The letters should be 1 inch high. Cut out the letters and iron them onto the center of the fabric. Design the rest of the fabric, drawing with the markers or ironing on more patches.

spring soup with teeny matzo balls

Matzo Balls:

5 tablespoons margarine

3 green onions, finely chopped

4 eggs

2 tablespoons chicken stock

2 teaspoons coarse kosher salt

1/4 teaspoon ground pepper

1 cup matzo meal

Soup:

1/4 cup vegetable oil

2 carrots, peeled and diced

2 small zucchini, diced

2 small yellow squash, diced

1 sweet potato, peeled and diced

1 cup fresh stemmed shiitake or
button mushrooms, quartered

4 shallots, chopped

4 garlic cloves, minced

6 cups chicken stock

1 can (28 ounces) diced
tomatoes, with juice

salt and pepper to taste

2 tablespoons chopped fresh basil

Passover is a spring holiday, so a fine way to celebrate this time of year is to feature updated chicken soup with seasonal vegetables. My friend Sandra adapted this recipe from one a friend gave her. She makes the matzo balls small so that they will be more delicate than typical ones. A good matzo ball is light and fluffy. There are many closely guarded secrets on how to achieve that, including beating the egg whites or adding seltzer water. Traditional versions use schmaltz, *or chicken fat.*

Serves 8

To make the matzo balls, melt the margarine over medium heat. Add the green onions and sauté for about 2 minutes. Let cool. In a large bowl, beat the eggs, stock, salt, and pepper. Mix in the matzo meal and green onions. Cover and chill until firm, at least 2 hours. Wet hands and roll small amounts of the matzo mixture (not quite a tablespoon each) into balls. Place on a baking sheet. Chill for 30 minutes. Bring a large pot of salted water to a boil. Drop the matzo balls into the boiling water, cover, and boil until the balls are tender, about 25 minutes. Using a slotted spoon, transfer the balls to a plate. These may be prepared in advance and kept refrigerated for 2 days.

To make the soup, heat the oil in a large, heavy saucepan over medium heat. Add the carrots, zucchini, squash, sweet potato, mushrooms, shallots, and garlic and sauté until almost tender, about 10 minutes. Add the stock and tomatoes with juice. Simmer over low heat until the vegetables are tender, about 20 minutes. Season with salt and pepper. Add the matzo balls to the soup and cook until heated through. Garnish with the basil. Serve in bowls.

lamb shanks with vegetables

Lamb is often traditionally eaten during Passover to commemorate the lamb sacrificed by the Jewish slaves of Egypt before they set out on the Exodus.

Serves 10 to 12

Rinse and dry the lamb shanks and sprinkle lightly with salt and pepper. Heat the oil in a large, heavy skillet over medium heat. Brown the shanks on all sides, about 5 minutes, and transfer to a platter. In the same skillet, sauté the garlic, onions, carrots, and celery until lightly browned, about 2 minutes.

Place the lamb shanks on top of the onion mixture. Add the wine and cook until reduced by half, 3 to 4 minutes. Add the tomatoes and juice, thyme, and parsley. Cover and simmer for 1 hour. Add the dried fruit. Continue cooking until the meat is tender enough to fall way from the bones, 30 to 60 minutes. Serve garnished with parsley.

12 lamb shanks, each 2 inches thick

salt and pepper to taste

$\frac{1}{2}$ cup vegetable oil

6 garlic cloves, minced

2 large onions, finely chopped

8 medium carrots, finely chopped

6 celery stalks, finely chopped

2 cups dry red wine

1 can (28 ounces) diced tomatoes, with juice

5 sprigs fresh thyme

$\frac{1}{4}$ cup chopped fresh parsley

1 cup (6 ounces) dried apricots or other dried fruit

fresh parsley for garnish

asparagus with garlic sauce

3 pounds medium asparagus

1 tablespoon salt

½ cup margarine

7 large garlic cloves, minced

1 tablespoon lemon juice

2 tablespoons Marsala

salt and pepper to taste

The first asparagus spears of the year are always welcome, and this sauce adds another flavor dimension to the beloved spring vegetable.

Serves 10 to 12

Snap off the base of each asparagus spear at the point it breaks naturally. Rinse under cold water. Fill a pot half full with water, add the 1 tablespoon salt, and bring to a boil. Slip the asparagus spears into the water, cover partially, and bring to a second boil. Uncover the pot and cook for 5 to 8 minutes. The asparagus should be tender and crisp and still bright green. Remove the asparagus and dry on a paper towel.

Meanwhile, melt the margarine in a small skillet over low heat. Add the garlic, lemon juice, and Marsala. Simmer until the garlic is lightly browned. Season with salt and pepper. Pour over the asparagus and serve.

new parsley potatoes

3 dozen small red potatoes, unpeeled and quartered

1 to 2 tablespoons olive oil

salt and pepper to taste

½ cup finely chopped fresh parsley

Traditionally, in Ashkenazic households, legumes and grains are not eaten during Passover because they can be ground into flour and used to make bread, which is prohibited. Potatoes, however, are acceptable, and these young red ones are featured in the spring festival.

Serves 10 to 12

Steam the potatoes over boiling water until tender, 10 to 15 minutes. Transfer to a large bowl. Add the olive oil and season with salt and pepper. Garnish with the parsley.

coconut pyramids of egypt

These edible pyramids replicate the magnificent structures of Egypt. And although the real pyramids were actually built hundreds of years before the Israelites were in Egypt, they evoke the history of the Jewish people in that land. Another popular traditional Passover treat, these confections taste like macaroons.

Yields approximately 45 pyramids

Preheat the oven to 350° F. Line a baking sheet with parchment.

In a large bowl, mix together the sugar, coconut, and egg whites. Add the margarine and extracts and mix well. Cover and refrigerate for at least 1 hour.

Dampen your hands. To make each pyramid, roll a tablespoon of the coconut mixture between your palms to form a compact ball. Place on a clean surface and flatten one side at a time, using a spatula to shape the pyramid. Place the pyramids on the baking sheet about 1 inch apart. Bake until the edges are golden brown, about 15 minutes. Let cool completely on the baking sheet.

Combine the chocolate and shortening in a small heatproof bowl and set over a pan of simmering water. Stir until melted. Dip the top ½ inch of each pyramid in the melted chocolate and place on the cooled baking sheet until the chocolate hardens.

1¾ cups sugar

5¼ cups unsweetened shredded coconut

7 large egg whites

2 tablespoons margarine, melted

1 teaspoon almond extract

1 teaspoon vanilla extract

4 ounces semisweet chocolate

½ teaspoon vegetable shortening

charoset

Soaked in sweet red wine, this ruby-colored combination of chopped apples and nuts symbolizes the mortar used by Jewish slaves to build the pyramids in Egypt. As with latkes, there are many recipes for this favorite dish. Some families chop the ingredients coarsely, while others make more of a paste. In every case, it should be prepared at least two hours in advance and refrigerated to allow the flavors to meld. The traditional recipes call for wine, but you can substitute grape juice.

basic charoset

2 red apples, unpeeled, cored, and finely chopped

1 cup finely chopped walnuts

2 tablespoons honey

1 teaspoon ground cinnamon

about ¼ cup sweet Passover wine

This is a common version of charoset, and it is the one my family makes for the holiday.

Yields 3 cups

Combine all the ingredients, using only as much wine as needed to bind the mixture. Serve in a bowl or roll into 1-inch balls and arrange on a serving plate.

78

sephardic charoset

The use of dried fruit distinguishes this as a Sephardic recipe. This version came from a friend's mother.

Yields 3 cups

In a medium pan, combine the dates, apples, and apricots. Add water to cover and bring to a boil over high heat. Lower the heat and simmer until the mixture is tender enough to mash with a fork, about 5 minutes. Remove from the heat, let cool slightly, and process in a blender, leaving some texture. Just before serving, fold in the walnuts.

½ cup pitted dates

2 cups peeled, cored, and thinly sliced apples

½ cup dried apricots

½ cup chopped walnuts

california charoset

Our family is always changing the charoset. Over the years, we have added such ingredients as pecans, dried papaya, dates, and prunes. It's fun to come up with a new version each year. We even had a charoset tasting, where all the guests at the Seder brought their own version of this Passover dish.

Yields 4 cups

Combine all the ingredients in a small bowl. Cover and refrigerate until serving.

3 apples, peeled, cored, and chopped

1 cup walnuts, toasted and chopped

¼ cup sunflower seeds, toasted

½ cup chopped dried apricots

¼ cup honey

3 tablespoons sweet Passover wine

1 teaspoon ground cinnamon

passover grape juice

1 bottle seltzer water

1 bottle grape juice

a piece of history

My Aunt Martha told me that when she lived in New York, she often went to the neighborhood candy store to get "two cents plain"— a glass of seltzer water for two cents. I remember her taking me to the store to get our own etched-glass bottle to take home. It was filled with carbonated water under high pressure, and when you pressed the handle on the bottle, the water shot out. It was great fun, and it made a fantastic whooshing noise that made anything you drank a blast. These bottles are hard to find now, but the search is worth the effort to find a piece of history.

During the Seder, we adults drink four cups of wine to symbolize the four promises of redemption in the Book of Exodus, while the children always get grape juice. We also use wine when we recite the plagues— blood, frogs, gnats, flies, cattle disease, boils, hail, locusts, darkness, and, finally, the death of the first-born—brought down on the Egyptians by God. Every time we read about a plague, we dip our fork into a glass, take it out, and scatter the drops of wine onto our plate as a symbol of regret that the victory had to be purchased through misfortune visited upon the Egyptians. In my family, when the last plague is recited, the one that finally convinced the Egyptians to let the Jews leave, we loudly clang our forks against our plates. Needless to say, young kids love this part of the Seder.

Serves 10 to 12

In a pitcher, mix together the seltzer water and grape juice to taste. Pour into wineglasses.

jumping paper frogs

According to the biblical story, Moses went to the pharaoh to demand the freedom of the Jews. He then threatened that God would bring the plagues to demonstrate His power and to punish the pharaoh for not letting them go. We make these paper frogs to decorate the Seder table as a reminder of one of those plagues. They also are fun to make with colorful origami paper.

For each frog you will need:

1 3-by-5-inch index card, or a piece of colored construction paper

paintbrush

green paint

❶ Fold the top edge of the card down to the left edge, and press the crease. Open the card flat.

❷ Fold the top edge the other direction toward the right edge. Open the card flat.

❸ Fold the card towards you, right where the creases cross. Open the card flat.

❹ Push down at 0. Bring X and Y together.

❺ Push down and flatten the triangle just formed on the front.

❻ Fold the outer corners of the triangle to the top corner (0).

❼ Fold the left and right edges of the card to the middle.

❽ Fold in half, bringing the bottom edge up to the point at the top (0).

❾ Fold the top edge of the front square down to the bottom edge. Sharpen the creases and turn over. You've made one frog. Tap the back of the frog and it'll jump.

❿ If you've used white card stock, paint the frog green and add 2 eyes on top.

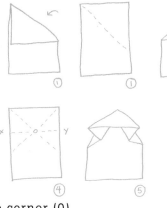

chocolate-dipped matzo

This is a fun and simple project to do with kids. You need only heat the chocolate for them; they can do their own dipping. And don't stop with matzo. Dried fruit, fresh strawberries, and nuts work well, too. As an alternative to dipping, use a teaspoon to dribble initials onto the matzo with the chocolate.

8 ounces semisweet chocolate

2 tablespoons water

1 one-pound box matzo

Yields about 24 matzo

Melt the chocolate with the water in a double boiler over hot water. Break the matzo in half or in smaller pieces. Dip the pieces into the chocolate, using tongs or fingers. Place the matzo pieces on waxed paper on a baking sheet. Refrigerate to harden.

chocolate torte

This cake is perfect for Passover because it uses no flour, yet is rich and simple to make. Kids love to beat the egg whites with a wire whisk.

oil and matzo meal for
  the cake pan

1½ cups blanched almonds

7 ounces bittersweet chocolate

1¼ cups sugar

7 egg whites

½ teaspoon almond extract

Yields 1 cake, serves 6 to 8

Preheat the oven to 300° F.

Oil a 9-inch springform pan and dust with matzo meal. Place the almonds and chocolate in a food processor and chop finely. Transfer to a large mixing bowl and add ¾ cup of the sugar. Mix well. Beat the egg whites with the remaining ½ cup sugar until stiff and shiny. Add the almond extract. Fold into the chocolate mixture and pour into prepared pan. Bake until firm, about 1 hour.

jake's matzo french toast

4 matzo squares

3 eggs

¼ cup (½ stick) butter

ground cinnamon to taste

sugar to taste

Growing up, my son, Jake, ate French toast almost every morning for breakfast. When it came time to celebrate Passover, we just switched from bread to matzo. This is my mom's recipe for matzo brei, *but changed to reflect Jake's passion for sugar and cinnamon. If you omit the cinnamon and sugar, it can be served with sour cream and thick jam, which is the way my mother served it. It's also delicious with sugared strawberries.*

Serves 4

In a colander, break up the matzo into 10 or 12 pieces. Over the sink, pour a teakettle full of hot water over the matzo pieces, making sure they all get wet. Using a fork, beat the eggs in a medium bowl until mixed. Put the wet matzo in the bowl of eggs and let it soak up the eggs. Heat the butter in a medium skillet. Add the matzo mixture and cook over medium heat, turning once, until crispy on both sides. The key to this recipe is butter, so use the full amount. When the matzo is almost done, sprinkle with cinnamon and sugar to taste.

Shavuot, which means "weeks" in Hebrew, is a holiday with many traditions and names. It is called Pentecost, Atzeret, the Holiday of Harvest, the Day of the First Fruits, and the Time of Giving of Our Torah. A spring harvest festival, it celebrates the shift from spring to summer. Israeli agricultural communities host a parade of tractors and of wagons and trucks filled with shepherds, gardeners, and dairy

shavuot, festival of weeks

workers, culminating in a festival where children sing, dance, and read poems. The holiday also represents the giving and the studying of the Torah, and some Jews stay up all night on Shavuot to study the Torah.

According to ancient tradition, a dairy meal is eaten at Shavuot because the new land where the Jews ended their trek was rich in milk and honey, as described in the Bible. For brunch, Cheese Blintzes, Farmers' Market Quiche, and New York Cheesecake fit the bill. Projects like the Shavuot Garden Box and the Covered Shavuot Journal commemorate both the spring harvest and the time of reflection.

covered shavuot journal

For each journal you will need:

blank book

scissors

sturdy fabric, such as felt,
in several colors to include
green and yellow

stencil brush

fabric glue

bone folder (available at
art-supply stores)

yellow embroidery thread

Because Shavuot is a time of reflection, a journal in which to write one's thoughts is a fitting project. This idea came from my nephew Mat, who is studying in Israel. He tells me that any activity that has to do with writing and reading is a good way to celebrate this holiday.

Open the book flat, with the pages facing down. Cut 1 piece of fabric to fit over the entire front and back cover spread, adding 2 inches on all sides.

Using the stencil brush, apply fabric glue to the front cover. Allow to dry for 30 seconds. Lay the fabric over the glue, centering the 2-inch border over and lining up any pattern on the fabric with the book's edges. Using the bone folder, press the fabric into the glue. Use the tip of the folder to push the fabric into the groove alongside the spine. Apply glue to the spine and back cover of the book. Pull fabric around and press into the second groove using the bone folder. Then smooth it onto the back of the book.

Open the front cover and notch the fabric at each corner of the book. Leave 1/8 inch of fabric at the point of the V to wrap over the corner. Apply glue on the inside cover edges, then fold remaining fabric inside and smooth it on the glue. Repeat for back cover edges. At the top and bottom of the spine, cut fabric down to 1/4 inch from the book's edge. Turn to the inside and glue flat.

To make felt leaves: Trace or draw a leaf shape onto paper and cut it out. Using the paper as a pattern, trace the leaf onto the green felt and use the scissors to cut it out. Pin the green felt leaf on yellow felt (or other contrasting color) and cut around the green leaf leaving a tiny border. Using yellow embroidery thread, stitch leaf veins with a basic running stitch. Attach to the covered journal with a bit of fabric glue.

farmers' market quiche

Shavuot is the traditional time when farmers brought their harvest to market. It thus seems appropriate to make a meal that includes fresh vegetables. A high-quality store-bought crust will do if you don't have time to make your own.

Serves 8

To make the crust, combine the butter, flour, and salt in a food processor. Process until crumbly, while slowly adding the water. When a soft ball forms, remove from the processor, wrap in aluminum foil, and refrigerate until firm, about 1 hour.

Preheat the oven to 350° F.

On a lightly floured surface, roll out the dough into a round about 1/8 inch thick. Don't bear down on the rolling pin; just move it away from the center in easy strokes. When the round is large enough, transfer it to a 9-inch pie pan. Trim away excess dough and crimp the edges. Using a fork, prick the bottom of the dough in several places and bake until golden brown, about 10 minutes. Let cool.

To make the filling, beat together the eggs, half-and-half, the 1/2 cup cheese, salt, pepper, and nutmeg. Place the broccoli and/or zucchini on the crust. Gently pour in the egg mixture. Sprinkle with the remaining 2 tablespoons of cheese. Bake until golden and set but not hard, about 25 minutes. Serve warm or at room temperature.

Crust:

1/3 cup plus 1 tablespoon butter

1 cup all-purpose flour

1/2 teaspoon salt

2 tablespoons water

Filling:

3 large eggs

1 1/2 cups half-and-half

1/2 cup plus 2 tablespoons grated Gruyère cheese

salt and pepper to taste

ground nutmeg to taste

3 cups chopped broccoli or zucchini, or a mixture

cheese blintzes

Blintzes remind me of French crepes, although they're Russian in origin. They can be filled with savory or sweet mixtures. Children have great fun mixing up the filling and stuffing the "pancakes." Serve these hot with sour cream topping, sliced strawberries, or stewed rhubarb (sweeten to taste or combine with canned crushed pineapple), or with applesauce on top of a sour cream dressing for additional garnish.

Yields 12 blintzes

To make the filling, in a bowl, combine the cheese, egg yolks, sugar, salt, and vanilla or cinnamon and stir with a fork until smooth and spreadable. If the cheese mixture is too thick, add the beaten egg whites or sour cream. If too thin, thicken with the cracker or bread crumbs, or mashed potatoes.

To make the batter, in a bowl, stir the sifted flour into the eggs and add the salt. Add the water gradually while beating; beat until free of lumps. Stir in the butter.

Starting at the center of a heated skillet greased with butter or non-stick spray, pour in the batter in a thin stream, tilting pan to spread the batter evenly. Cook over low heat when starting, increasing heat as soon as the pancake is smooth and firm on top and the bottom is lightly browned. Turn out onto a double layer of paper towels, bottom side up, and spread evenly with 1 tablespoon of the filling. While each successive pancake is in the skillet, the preceding blintz can be filled and rolled up, tucking in the ends. When all the blintzes are done, add more butter to the skillet and brown the blintzes lightly on both sides until firm.

Filling:

1 pound dry cottage cheese, or mixed cream cheese and farmer cheese, in any proportion

2 egg yolks

1 tablespoon sugar

dash of salt

several drops of vanilla extract or dash of ground cinnamon

1 egg white, beaten, or 1 tablespoon sour cream (optional)

1 tablespoon fine cracker or white bread crumbs, or mashed potatoes (optional)

Batter:

1 cup sifted all-purpose flour

2 eggs, beaten

pinch of salt

1½ cups water, or half milk and half water

2 tablespoons butter, melted, plus additional butter for frying

new york cheesecake

Crust:

1¼ cups graham cracker crumbs

1 tablespoon sugar (optional)

¼ cup (½ stick) unsalted butter or margarine, melted

Filling:

2 cups (1 pint) sour cream

1 cup plus 1 tablespoon sugar

2½ teaspoons vanilla extract

3 packages (24 ounces) cream cheese, at room temperature

4 eggs

Cheesecake is almost always served on Shavuot. A dairy meal is eaten on the first day to symbolize the saying in the Bible, "And He gave us this land flowing with milk and honey." Preparing dairy dishes has also been traced to the custom of serving a meal to those who studied the Torah all night.

Serves 10 to 12

Preheat the oven to 350° F.

To make the crust, in a large bowl, thoroughly blend the crumbs, sugar (if using), and melted butter. Spoon the mixture evenly into a 9-inch springform pan until it's halfway up the sides and press it down firmly. Refrigerate for at least 15 minutes and then bake until set, 10 minutes. Set aside to cool completely.

To make the filling, beat the sour cream and 1 tablespoon of the sugar in a bowl. Add 1 teaspoon of the vanilla extract and beat until well blended. Set aside. In the bowl of an electric mixer, beat the cream cheese with the remaining 1 cup sugar until light and fluffy. Add the eggs, one at a time, mixing well after each addition. Beat in the remaining vanilla extract. Pour this filling into the prepared crust.

Bake until the center is set and the top is golden brown, about 50 minutes. Remove from the oven. Spread the prepared sour cream mixture on top and return to the oven for 5 minutes to set. Remove from the oven, let cool, cover, and refrigerate for 24 hours. Remove from the pan. Serve chilled or at room temperature.

rubber band printed stationery

This is a fun way to create your own stationery. Read the Torah and write down the thoughts it inspires on the stationery. Share this inspiration with friends or relatives.

Cover one side of a wooden block with the tape (you may need more than one piece). Trim off any excess. Don't remove the peel-off backing yet.

Use the scissors to cut several rubber bands of the same type into pieces of different sizes. Arrange the pieces on a table until you have a design you like. Don't overlap the bands, and use the same type for each block. Remove the backing from the tape. Piece by piece, adhere your design to the sticky tape. Trim off any pieces that don't fit on the block. Your stamp is ready to use. Make additional stamps in the same way.

Press a stamp on a pad a few times, or use the markers to "paint" the stamp. Be sure you get an even coat on the stamp. Put a magazine under your stationery to create a firm work surface. Practice a few times on scrap paper by pressing down firmly and evenly. When you're ready to print, stamp around the edges of the plain stationery to make a border.

If you want to use the same stamp with different colors, clean it by pressing it down onto a damp paper towel a few times. Then press it onto a dry paper towel. Let the stamp dry before you try a second color.

small blocks of wood of any shape, 1 to 3 inches long

two-sided tape with peel-off backing

scissors

rubber bands of various widths

stamp pads with washable ink, or washable markers in various colors

scrap paper

plain stationery, envelopes, and note cards

shavuot garden box

On Shavuot, the house is decorated with greenery, since the holiday celebrates the earth's bounty. Your kids can make these cute garden boxes to brighten up the kitchen table.

To make the fence, lay two Popsicle sticks about 1 1/4 inches apart. Lay five sticks perpendicular to them on top; spread evenly, and glue. Make three more fences in this manner and let them dry. On the long strip of cardboard, use the pencil to mark and the knife to score four equal sections. Each should be 4 1/4 inches wide. Fold the strip into a box shape and tape the ends together. Tape the cardboard square to the bottom of the box.

Cover the box with green construction paper by cutting four 4 1/2-inch-wide side pieces and gluing them on; make the height of the side pieces taller than the box and cut the top to look like bushes, if you like. Paint flowers along the bottom edge of the side pieces, or cut out pictures of flowers from magazines or seed catalogs and glue them on the side pieces.

Lay the box on its side and apply glue to one section of the fence. Place the fence on the box and let dry before turning the box and attaching the other sections in the same way. Fill with a pot full of flowers.

For each box you will need:

28 Popsicle or craft sticks, painted white

all-purpose white glue

1 piece corrugated cardboard, 2 1/4 by 17 inches

pencil

utility knife

masking tape

1 piece corrugated cardboard, 4 1/2 inches square

6 sheets green construction paper

scissors

paint

paintbrush

magazines or seed catalogs with pictures of flowers (optional)

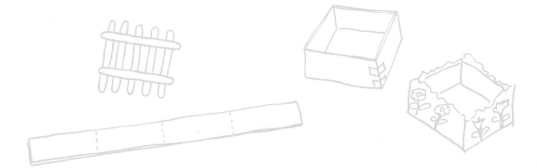

index